10 MENTAL HACKS FOR YOUR PANIC ATTACKS

TOM WARD

Copyright © Tom Ward 2019

All rights reserved. No part of this publication may be reproduced, stored in a retrieval system, or transmitted in any form or by any means, electronic, mechanical, photocopying, recording or otherwise, without the prior written permission of the copyright owner.

The content of this book is provided for informational and entertainment purposes only. It is not intended to be used as medical advice or as a substitute for proper medical evaluation or treatment by a qualified health care professional. All information is believed to be accurate as presented, based on the author's own research, however, neither the author nor the publisher guarantees the accuracy, quality, suitability or reliability of any information contained herein.

TABLE OF CONTENTS

Preface i

Introduction 1

I Think, Therefore I Am... Afraid 5

Dog Training 101 11

Fighting Fire With Fire 15

Rocky vs The Karate Kid 19

The Beatles vs Bizarro World 23

Tell Spock It Worked 27

Alchemical Magic 31

Please ~~Don't~~ Interrupt 35

Be Here Now (or at least by next Tuesday) 41

Symbols 47

Afterword 49

APPENDIX: Mental Hack Action Steps 52

PREFACE

It was approximately 4:30 in the morning when I dialed 9-1-1. I work an early shift and get up around 4 o'clock each workday morning. This was my first major panic attack but I didn't know that at the time; I just thought I was going to die. After the phone call, I packed a small carry-on bag. I was certain that they would, at least, cut open my chest and I would probably have to be in the hospital for a while. That is, if I didn't die.

Twelve hours later, I was released from the hospital. I wasn't dying, to my relief. That's the good news. The bad news: the bill for my 12 hour stay was $10,271.04 including $624 for the several mile ambulance ride. More good news, I had insurance. More bad news: a $4000 out-of-pocket deductible.

Four thousand dollars. That's some motivation to find some answers. I'm an admitted information junkie and I love research. I gathered some valuable information about panic attacks.

Some things surprised me along the way like the Canadian study that found positive affirmations only help people with high self-esteem. Seems to me that they're the folks that need it the least.

Anyway, the more I learned about panic attacks, the more I realized *how I looked at them* made all the difference in the world.

What follows is my viewpoint on what I learned.

I hope it helps.

INTRODUCTION

What do you see in this picture? Hint: it's an animal.

If you've seen this before then you certainly know the answer.

Oliver Wendell Holmes, Jr. said, "man's mind, once stretched by a new idea, never regains its original dimensions." If you've *never* seen this before try to find the "hidden object".

It's an interesting fact that when a human fetus is formed the cells form the brain first followed by the spinal cord -- our nervous system. Without this our bodies are essentially useless clods of flesh, hence the term *brain dead* when a comatose brain ceases to operate. It is through this system that we interpret our environment. Through our senses we take in elements of our outer environment and our brain interprets what we see, hear, touch, smell and taste.

A remarkable system to be sure but one subject to a myriad of interpretations depending on the personal input of the individual.

Would someone looking at a postcard of Manhattan who has visited the city many times have the same impact as someone who has never left her hometown? Of course not.

How about someone about to taste a mango for the first time compared to someone who has tasted its intense sweetness many times before? Again, the experiences *must* be different.

Our brains are constantly interpreting incoming stimuli that we then "digest" and store as "facts". However, there is a "ghost in the machine" that puts an individual spin on these "facts" and unfortunately for some of us -- especially panic attack sufferers -- that ghost is scary indeed.

Wishing may not "make it so" but sometimes just thinking does. In our mind, at least. We convince ourselves that these sensations we are feeling are real -- we *know* they are!

But *are* they real?

For some panic attack sufferers, all it takes to relieve perhaps decades of fear is a paradigm shift in thinking -- a radical change in long-held thought patterns that allow us to see things in a different way.

Like the shifting of tectonic plates deep beneath the earth's crust, the resulting shift leaves a permanent change in how we view our fears.

Vision is one of the processes we use to interpret the stimuli we take in. Did you see the cow in the picture? Once you do -- like an "aha moment" -- you always will.

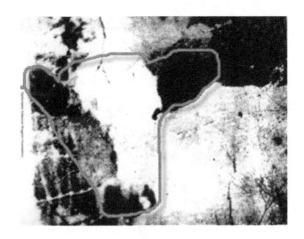

Now let's see if we can **"hack"** your mind in a way so that you see your panic for what it really is.

Tom Ward

I THINK, THEREFORE I AM... AFRAID

French philosopher Descartes is credited with saying "I think, therefore I am." What we want to consider now is the idea that **your thoughts cause your emotions**.

The fear and panic you experience during a panic attack is caused by your thoughts and not the result of any outside stimuli. So changing your thoughts will change your feelings.

Let's try an experiment: think for a moment of the person you love the most -- mother, father, your spouse, child, whomever. Let those thoughts wash over you. Imagine embracing that person and hearing them say, "I love you." HEAR their VOICE saying it to you.

Now keeping those thoughts in mind, imagine you are at work or school and you get an emergency phone call. The speaker on the other end tells you that there has been a terrible accident involving your loved one and that you need to get home immediately. "What happened," you ask, "are they all right?" They repeat "JUST GET HOME NOW!" Distraught and in a daze, you race passed your boss or teacher and mumble that there's an emergency and you have to leave immediately. The ride home is painful, filled with anxiety. The caller was insistent so it must be a worst case scenario.

As you arrive home you throw open the front door and

standing there -- healthy as ever -- is the loved one about whom you had imagined the worst. Forget whether this was a cruel practical joke devised to get you home or that there is a simple, logical explanation for the caller's actions. Just ask yourself: what caused you to feel so despondent? It wasn't *the fact* that your loved one was injured or worse because s(he) wasn't.

It was *the thought* that great harm or worse had come to your loved one. Our thoughts create our feelings.

Here's another one: this morning at 9 a.m. you're scheduled to give the most important presentation of your life. The company's CEO and several potential investors will be attending your meeting. You've prepared for this for weeks but you're not sure you can pull it off. Not only may your position with the company be at stake, but the company itself, since the investors' "yea or nay" will decide the company's financial fate.

You've done your homework. You know your numbers are solid and your boss chose you because of your years of proven competency. But you haven't slept at all the last two days and although your husband has been supportive -- almost to a fault -- you're not sure you can pull it off

Your husband sneaks down to the kitchen early while you're tossing and turning and prepares your favorite breakfast.

You roll over and are greeted by him holding a breakfast tray ready to place it over your lap "you look beautiful," he says, "how do you do that so early in the morning?" (And where ever did he get that single rose in the vase perched on the corner of the breakfast tray?)

You're not the least bit hungry but you manage to down a few bites because you know the trouble he went through.

You shower, primp and dress in that new suit you bought for the occasion remembering to remove the price tags.

As you're headed out the door your husband says, "you're gonna knock it out of the park. I *know* you are." He then plants the softest kiss you ever felt in your entire life smack dab on your lips.

At work you skip the morning coffee -- you're wired enough -- and head down the long corridor to the main conference room. It's ten minutes to nine. You're thinking how the corridor doesn't seem as long as it usually does as your stomach is doing flip-flops when your cell phone hums from your jacket pocket.

You lift it out and read the ID -- it's your husband. "Honey, you are NOT going to BELIEVE this. I just checked the numbers on last nights Mega Millions. We won! We won!"

"What," you say stunned.

"We won! A hundred and seventy million dollars! I just called in sick. Let's keep this under the radar until we can talk to a lawyer and financial planner. You okay?"

"Okay? Yeah, yeah... I'm great."

"Oh, and good luck with the meeting. I love you."

You're in front of the meeting room. You don't remember saying goodbye to your husband, pocketing the phone or walking into the conference room. What you do know is that you feel AMAZING. Like years of stress melted off in an instant. Hell, you could "knock it out of the park" if you looked like Krusty the Clown but you, in your new suit and looking "beautiful" (and so early in the morning. How *do* I *do* that! You wonder.)

Well, you not only hit it out of the park but into the next stadium. After the *postmortem meeting* your boss tells you to take the rest of the day off. "Go to the spa, you earned it. We can talk about your raise and promotion tomorrow."

Well, you can probably see where we're headed. Yeah, your husband lied to you about winning the lottery, the little sh*t (just wanted you to be "up' for the meeting). But not about being beautiful and knocking it out of the park. You're not sure if you want to strangle him or give him the sloppiest kiss you can muster. One thing for sure... your THOUGHTS caused your FEELINGS.

Winning the lottery didn't melt your anxiety away like ice on a hot plate. THINKING you won the lottery did.

Our thoughts create our feelings.

MENTAL HACK ONE ACTION STEP: Think of at least two times when *your* thoughts caused your feelings.

Tom Ward

DOG TRAINING 101

Ivan Pavlov, a Russian scientist (actually he deserves to have it mentioned that he was a triple-threat: physiologist, psychologist, and physician) did extensive studies in the late 1800s and early 1900s on what has come to be known as the "conditioned response" or, in his own words, the *conditional reflex*.

His work on reflex actions involved involuntary reactions to stress and pain and the phrase "Pavlov's dog" is often used to describe someone who merely reacts to a situation rather than using critical thinking.

Pavlov would ring a bell each time before feeding his dog and the dog would salivate as a response to the food. After repeated practice, however, the dog began to salivate in response to the bell alone.

Unfortunately, this is what many panic attack suffers now do habitually as a result of these involuntary reflexes – feeling equals fear equals *panic*.

We're all conditioned to some degree by stimuli in our environment. This is a throwback to our *primitive* brain and, in some cases, still critical to our survival. That loud noise you hear may *not* be the growl of a saber-toothed tiger but it *may* be the side of your Volvo gently scraping the expressway guardrail as you nod off on that long trip to grandma's house. Fear does have its advantages. So the practice of medicating our fears away may, in fact, be dangerous in itself. Self-medicating with alcohol or so-called "recreational drugs" is unquestionably foolish and ultimately destructive.

You've probably "seen" or at least heard of the "invisible fence" that's used to train dogs to stay within a certain defined area. If the dog runs *through* the "fence" he's zapped with a somewhat mild jolt of electrical current that stops him in his tracks.

Like a stunned animal, many of us, at the onset of a panic attack, become one of "Pavlov's dogs" and merely react to our situation rather than using logical thought. Our primitive (animal) brain has won out. We *react instinctively* rather than judge the degree of danger we're confronted with. The poor dog can't reason his way around this one – but *you* can!

The next time a panic attack hits, THINK first, then, and only then, REACT to what your logical (human) brain is telling you rather than letting your automatic reaction (your animal brain) control the situation. Your body is telling you *"this has happened before, I know what to do."* You've hit that "invisible fence" before and, by golly, you don't need anybody or anything to tell you how to react. You've already done an excellent job of erecting that "fence" and training yourself.

Now it's time for your human brain to step up and show who's the boss.

Am I asking you to tear down the "fence" that you've built? No…. something even scarier. I'm asking you to *embrace* it!

That's right. **Grab hold of that electrified fence and don't let go.**

MENTAL HACK TWO ACTION STEP: Think of specific actions you take throughout your day that are actually re-actions.

Tom Ward

FIGHTING FIRE WITH FIRE

You may have read or heard the saying that "you can't fight anxiety with more anxiety" and maybe the analogy of struggling to free yourself from Chinese handcuffs was used to illustrate the point. At first, this seems logical, but remember, we're not dealing with our "logical brain."

Sometimes we need to fight fire with fire!

Have you ever heard of the term *backburning*? It's a method sometimes used by firefighters to help control wildfires. Here's how it works: Typically, it involves controlling the area that the fire can spread to by removing dead trees and debris, creating "control lines" that are areas that contain no combustible material. These control lines can be produced by bulldozing, or by backburning — setting a small, low-intensity fire to burn the flammable material in a controlled way. These may then be extinguished by firefighters, *or,* **ideally, directed in such a way so that <u>they meet the main fire front, at which point both fires will run out of flammable material and be extinguished.</u>**

When dealing with our "animal brain" sometimes what seems intuitive and logical will keep us trapped in a repetitive cycle.

This "fighting fire with fire" or "fighting anxiety with MORE anxiety" is exactly what's being employed in the very promising work done with Intensive Exposure Therapy. The therapist coaxes the patient into *confronting* the "high anxiety" instead of fearing it.

As Ralph Waldo Emerson has promised: ***Do the thing you fear,*** **and the death of fear is certain.**

However, when "fighting fire with fire" pyromaniacs need not apply.

Let me explain... In our above short paragraph explaining *backburning,* the word, or a form of the word, "control" was used FIVE times. That's tied for the number one spot for word usage in the paragraph (and that includes "the" & "a"). Seems pretty important, wouldn't you say?

Controlling the energy of a panic attack is essential. Rather than letting your "attacker" attack you, you wage a strategic attack on *it*. You're in for a fight.

You often hear people talk about "fighting" their phobias or "battling" their panic attacks and, after all is said and done, it does seen like a pretty decent analogy with all the energy that's expended.

So if we're in for a fight, why not fight **to win**?

MENTAL HACK THREE ACTION STEPS: Think of how you react to a panic attack. Is it the same way each time? Have you ever devised a plan to "fight back"? You are being "attacked" after all.

Watch as a young agoraphobic woman confronts her fear of elevators during a session of Intensive Exposure Therapy:

On *YouTube* Search "Intensive Exposure Therapy" and choose the first entry (6:16 minutes).

Note: Actual urls for all web links are listed in the Appendix and are active in the digital version.

Tom Ward

ROCKY VS THE KARATE KID

Ever watch a heavyweight prizefight? Yeah, to be honest, I'm not really big on watching two grown men (or women) beat each other senseless. But in the context of a movie like *Rocky*, it fits the bill

So, you have two opponents, each using **brute force**, trying to overcome the other.

One of the greatest boxers of all times was Muhammad Ali. Despite what may be said about Ali's "psychological tactics," his ability to win a fight amounted to little more than fast hands, dance-like moves and the ability to give *and take* a severe blow to the face. In short, **brute force**, except for that dancing part, of course.

On the other hand, I find watching a martial arts (karate, kung fu, jujitsu, etc.) bout fascinating. Here, something much more interesting than brute force is going on.

Instead of your ability to withstand a crushing blow to the face, what becomes crucial is your ability to use your opponent's energy against him. Your opponent swings, and instead of either absorbing the blow or avoiding it, you sidestep it *and* <u>use your opponent's energy (i.e. forward motion) to your advantage.</u>

Imagine someone *charging* at you. At the last possible moment, you step aside, turn, and as they pass you, you place your hands on their back and push. **KABLAM!!!** In the *dirt*!

This is what you *must* do when a panic attack strikes if you're going to break the cycle. Use the energy of the attack *against* the attack itself. You're in for a fight, SO FIGHT!

Get *serious*!

"You wanna piece of me? **You** wanna a piece of **me**? Well bring it! I'm not afraid of you anymore. Come on! "

If you're into profanities, use them. You're mad as hell and you're not gonna take it anymore!

Now, hopefully you're alone when this happens and not in your neighborhood grocery store. (Of course, you can always whip out your cell phone and hold it to your ear. Everyone will just think you having an argument…. No, I'm just kidding).

If you *are* in public, get to your car or somewhere else that you feel safe and do it. Or do it mentally.

You're familiar with positive affirmations. How about using this as a new twist. Call it your "I'll kick your ass-firmation!" Next time a panic attack strikes, think Robert De Niro in "Taxi Driver" and hit it with a "you talkin' to me? You talkin' to *me*? Well I'm the only one here."

Pssssst! Lean in closely; I have something important to tell you. Here's the best-kept secret about panic attacks. They're two-bit cheap punk thugs. Nothing but a bunch of bullies. *And when you confront them? They crumble to dust like a childhood boogeyman.*

Go get'em, tiger!

MENTAL HACK FOUR ACTION STEPS: Get some inspiration from Frank Costanza and De Niro's Travis Bickle (WARNING: Adult language!)

On *YouTube* Search "You talking to me - Robert De Niro" and choose the (0:32minutes) entry.

On *YouTube* Search "You Want A Piece of Me?" for the Seinfeld entry at (0:59minutes).

Tom Ward

LET IT BE

THE BEATLES VS BIZARRO WORLD

Let's get back to that Chinese handcuffs analogy for a moment.

Some people will have you believe that in the midst of a panic attack you should r-e-l-a-x. When you get anxious, instead of tensing, let go. Instead of fighting harder you should relax. Or like the words of the Beatles' song, you should LET IT BE. *Let it be, let it be, let it be, let it be....* Now I'll admit that there are times when these are, indeed, "words of wisdom" but when you're having a panic attack? I'm not so sure.

Ever have someone tell you to "just relax" when you having a panic attack? I don't know about you but my reaction would undoubtedly be the same one hundred percent of the time. I might not say it but I sure would be thinking it.... *"No sh*t, Sherlock! If I could do that, I wouldn't be in this position now would I?"*

Now I don't mean to come off as an ingrate, I honestly do appreciate anyone that has the compassion to help a fellow human being in need but telling someone that's having a panic attack to "just relax" is like telling someone that's on fire to "stay cool."

If I could, I would.

"Breathe deeply" or "is there anything I can do for you?" are thoughtful and appropriate. But "relax" just doesn't do it for me.

With the Chinese handcuffs, if pulling doesn't work, and actually makes things worse, then try pushing, right? Makes sense. But with a panic attack, haven't you already *tried* to relax? I mean like <u>every time</u>, right? It's a no-brainer, the logical thing to do. If you're tense, you should try to relax. Trouble is, it hasn't worked. Right? Or why would you be wasting your time reading this when you could be reading….

A comic book?

I'll forgive anyone reading this who isn't a fan of *Superman* comics but for guys growing up in simpler times, it was a rite of passage.

There was a planet called "the Bizarro World" or "Htrae," which is "Earth" spelled backwards, in case you didn't catch that. This cubed-shaped planet had a code, aptly called the Bizarro Code, which states in simple terms what its inhabitants must do: "Us do opposite of all Earthly things! Us hate beauty! Us love ugliness! Is big crime to make anything perfect on Bizarro World!"

So, in short, whatever we do on Earth, they do the opposite on Bizarro World. So, now the time has come. You've tried it their way. You tried to *relax*. You tried to "Let It Be" and where has it gotten you? Still searching, right?

Forget those Chinese Handcuffs! **Welcome to the Bizarro World!**

Instead of trying to relax, let 'em have it. Ya gotta up the ante. Fight 'em the Chicago way. Hit 'em with both barrels. Think Sean Connery's Jim Malone in "The Untouchables": You wanna get the panic attack? Here's how you get him. He pulls **knife**, you pull a **gun**…."

We have to break the cycle, so the old way of doing things just doesn't work.

Show the bully what you're made of.

MENTAL HACK FIVE ACTION STEPS: Think of how you can react differently at the onset of your next panic attack in order to break an habitual cycle.

Listen to Jim Malone's Chicago Strategy:

On *YouTube* Search "The Chicago Way" for the (0:09 minutes) entry.

TELL SPOCK IT WORKED

I'm a big Star Trek fan. Not geeky enough to dress up like a Klingon and go to conventions but a big fan. Mostly of the original series although I'm the first to admit that **any** of the series that followed (The Next Generation, Voyager, Deep Space Nine, etc.) had far better production value. The budget for the original had to be pretty slim since the "special effects" are like something an eleven-year-old kid with a cheap laptop could outdo today. But the stories -- WOW!

They tackled some of the great themes that continue to excite us since the Greek dramatists first put quill to papyrus -- prejudice, human rights, religion, war and peace, personal loyalty and on and on.

One continuing theme was that of an "alien presence" that affected the crew and caused them to somehow act differently than their usual selves. Whether that "difference" was happier, sadder, more courageous or more fearful inevitably depended on deep-seated beliefs held by the characters.

Are you holding any deep-seated beliefs that affect your behavior? Do you believe that your panic attacks are a part of you that you have to live with or learn to tame?

Maybe we can take a page from a Star Trek script and use it to our advantage.

Imagine an "alien entity" has entered your "personal space."

This alien wants you to act afraid because for some reason his sorry butt gets a kick out of it. (Maybe it's an alien child like "General Trelane, Retired" in Star Trek's *The Squire of Gothos*).

Now as long as you see this fear as something emanating from *within* you then you may see it as something you **have to live with**. But imagine for a moment you see this bully for what it really is -- not something from within you -- but something outside of you -- something trying to **control** you. To make you afraid. To rob you of your strength and courage.

Now you have something you can sink your teeth into. Something you can fight or... if you choose... something you can befriend.

In English literature, there's a figure of speech called "personification" in which an inanimate object or an abstraction is endowed with human qualities or represented as having a human form -- like raindrops *dancing* on a still pond.

The more you can see your panic or anxiety as being something outside of you -- an alien force -- the closer you will come to understand that you have complete control of it.

When your panic attack strikes, see it not as coming from within you but as a concrete, physical entity. Make it look like anything you want. Maybe something really silly so you can laugh at it instead of being afraid.

Does your panic attack look like a clown? A collie pup? A wolf? No? Maybe a teddy bear... or even your kid sister. No? Maybe it should.

Make it look like a kind and ordinary man if you'd like. Like the great and powerful "Wizard of Oz" hiding his true nature behind a bag of tricks. That's really what it is. Make it look like the Tin Man or the Cowardly Lion.

But make it look like **something** – anything. Or anybody. Put a tag on it; give it a name. Good or evil? That's up to you.

Are you a warrior, a negotiator, a lover? What's your strength – your modus operandi? You're in control now.

Now that it's visible you have a target. Shoot it or hug it.

Your panic attacks control you only because you see no other way. It's time to start looking at them differently. Come up with your own "technology" to trick this alien beast.

Then, when the alien is dismissed, you can smile and whisper to yourself, "tell Spock it worked."

MENTAL HACK SIX ACTION STEPS: Watch what happens when an alien takes over the Enterprise and how it is defeated:

On *YouTube* Search "Star Trek and its Solution to Drummed Up Hatred" at (4:32 minutes).

Does your panic attack look like this alien:

On *YouTube* Search "Star Trek - Attack of the Parasites" at (2:05 minutes).

Time to see the light:

On *YouTube* Search "Star Trek - Seeing the Light" at (1:51 minutes).

What does your panic attack LOOK like?

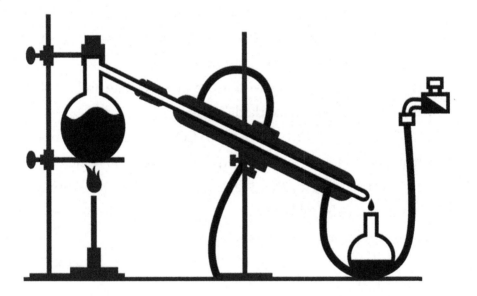

ALCHEMICAL MAGIC

In the branch of magic known as alchemy the ultimate goal of the magician/alchemist is to transmute a base metal, such as lead, into a precious metal, such as gold.

Science has proved what the ancients already knew: matter and energy never die, they only change.

So what's this got to do with panic attacks? Maybe some much-needed relief.

In the transmuting process from ice to water, in its natural environment, ice first turns to slush and then water. So slush is in a "closer state" to ice, sharing its chemical components as well as temperature.

Now, when a panic attack strikes, our mental/emotional state is one of fear and our logical brain is trying to "transmute" this fear into calm. If you instead embrace this fear and try to transmute it into excitement, say the thrill of your favorite amusement park ride rather than directly into calm, you may find your job a bit easier. After your "roller coaster ride" you can step off and actually feel exhilarated rather than physically worn out.

It's easier to transmute directly from one arousal state to another rather than directly to a state of calm. Like ice and slush sharing a similar temperature, fear and exhilaration share similar states of physical arousal.

So you ask: just how do you perform this magical feat? Well, for most of us, at the onset of a panic attack we are almost always conscious of a change in bodily sensations – a rapid heartbeat, tightening in the chest, or dizziness. And then our doom filled thoughts. *"Oh no, not again!"*

At the first sign of this physical change we borrow another technique from the magician -- imagination. The creative power of the mind. You close your eyes and form a mental image of the most wildly conceived thrill ride your imagination can conjure. The tallest, fastest, curviest, scariest ride you can imagine. Or maybe, with closed eyes, you see that unreachable heartthrob asking you out on a date? Anything that will get your juices flowing. (You may want to practice this "imagining" when you're in a relaxed state many times until it's routine. This is referred to as "mental rehearsal.")

Have your "roller coaster ride" picked out in advance, **roll with it**, and *whammo*, it's magic!

What we resist persists.

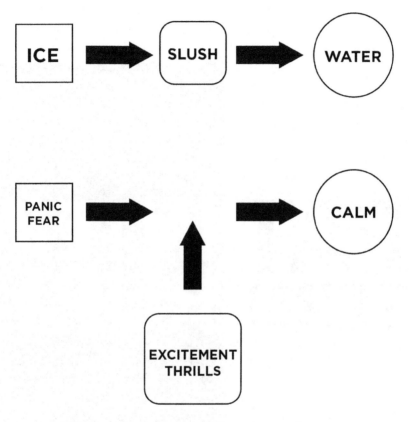

What we mentaly embrace, we chase.

MENTAL HACK SEVEN ACTION STEP: Use your imagination to come up with an exciting scenario that you can use to transmute your next panic attack.

Tom Ward

PAT TERN INTER RUPT

PLEASE ~~DON'T~~ INTERRUPT

The average human being is like a zombie. Not a "Walking Dead" zombie but one that has voluntarily switched their mental capacities from conscious to unconscious control.

Let's face it – all of us have our days filled with mundane activities: brushing our teeth, walking the dog, driving to work, dressing for school, *ad infinitum*.

We're on autopilot when we do these things. We've done them so often that they don't require thought, just zombie-like action. Over the years our repetitive motions have actually changed how our brains operate. We've created *neural pathways* in our brains to make our step-by-step processes easier to traverse.

When you hop on a bicycle, you don't have to think what to do because your brain created a path to easily follow. And you've done it so often that you created a pattern to follow. We've become so proficient in these tasks that they don't need any conscious thought.

This is true of panic attack victims who have suffered for years molding a precise pattern like the grooves of an old record album (for Millennials: these flat plastic discs came before MP3s, cassettes and 8-track tapes. Check with grandpa, he may still have some).

Your job now as a panic attack sufferer is to first, take notice of your pattern. Try to consciously remember what you experience at the onset of a panic attack and then carry it through the building up process to a full-blown attack.

Do you get lightheaded? Feel otherworldly? Does your heart begin to race? Does your breathing become shallow? Try to bring it to the very first occurrence that you know you are having a panic attack.

This is your launch site for your *Pattern Interrupt*. You are going to interrupt your habitual, autopilot moves that lead to your panic attack and throw the bully off course.

We must know our enemy's moves precisely to build our strategy. We must "steal" the competitors "playbook" and know his moves completely.

No matter what the sport, you must always study the competition. Coaches watch hours upon hours of the competition's plays in order to develop a strategy.

If a boxing coach knows that his boxer's competition has a habit of throwing **two right jabs**, followed by **a left jab** then followed by a *power punching* **uppercut**, he can use this knowledge against the opponent.

Once you know what "triggers" the onset of the attack you can disrupt the normal pattern.

Say your pattern is: feeling lightheaded, followed by shallow breathing, then rapid heartbeat and thoughts like "Not again! Oh no, please! Am I dying?" then pacing the floor and hyperventilating.

So, just at the moment you begin to feel lightheaded, this is the moment you trigger your *Pattern Interrupt*.

What should your *Pattern Interrupt* be? That's up to you, think **big** though. The more outlandish the better chance of it being effective.

If you could have a bucket of ice water dropped over your head this might be extremely effective but maybe you'll have to settle for splashing cold water on the face. Maybe breaking out singing a Broadway show tune, particularly one you hate. Dancing the Irish jig while humming an accompanying tune. Or performing a ninja-like jujitsu move with a "Ha! Ha! Haaaa!" Be physical. Use your breath. Remember, the crazier the better.

Now that's strategy one. We're building our playbook. Next, what happens if you're in a public place? You may be able to make it to your car but if not, you'll need a different *Pattern Interrupt*. Plan it in advance. If you sometimes have an attack at the grocery store and you usually abandon your cart and head for the door maybe you rapidly walk the aisles in the opposite direction than you usually take as if looking for something while internally singing a nursery rhyme. Plan ahead imagining the sequences. Develop your *Pattern Interrupt*; be prepared to meet the enemy.

Important: don't mix strategies. The one you developed to use at home, use it at home. If you can use it everywhere, so much the better. But if your at home strategy differs from your away from home strategy, don't mix them.

It may take several tries to break your pattern just as a simple scratch on that old record album might not be enough to damage the groove. You want to apply this new pattern to break the old pattern your habit-induced brain "helped" you create. **Repeated new input equals new pathway.**

Be consistent. Be determined. Believe.

But wait! There's a glitch: the time between our trigger and the response from our amygdala, the fear center of our primitive brain, happens in the blink of an eye. How can we break this chain reaction.

Mind.... If I continue?

MENTAL HACK EIGHT ACTION STEP: Devise your two *Pattern Interrupt* scenarios. One for when you're in the public and one when you're alone.

Tom Ward

BE HERE NOW (OR AT LEAST BY NEXT TUESDAY)

We are not in control of our mind.

We think we are but a simple observation of our thoughts will prove otherwise. We're inattentive to our thoughts – mindless rather than mindful. Our lives have become routine, again that zombie-like behavior that we've adopted from years of practice.

We think (and most often worry) about the past and the future. What we did and what we still must do. But **the past and future do not exist**. The past is gone and the future has not yet arrived. The only time that matters, really matters, is the time that we can do something about our situation, our problems, our lives.

That time is NOW!

Take a few minutes to observe your thoughts and you'll find that your mind jumps about uncontrolled. The mind has been described by some as a "drunken monkey" or "an unbroken horse" moving to and fro without direction or control. And where does this rudderless movement lead us?

Centuries ago The Buddha said, "Whatever an enemy might do to an enemy, or a foe to a foe, the ill-directed mind can do to you even worse."

Our habitual thinking has brought us to our present state but fortunately for us **our minds are plastic and malleable**. If we begin to take control, we can shape our minds, change our thoughts, thereby changing our emotions. Remember our thoughts create our emotions.

At 7 AM on December 10, 1996 Harvard trained brain scientist Jill Bolte Taylor had a massive stroke in the left hemisphere of her brain. Our left brain processes incoming information and our right brain controls our sensory system: the sights, sounds, smells, tastes and touch of the present moment; our left brain is concerned with the past and the future, with language, logic and the ego. Our right brain sees pictures and hears sounds of the now – only the present.

Dr. Taylor's right brain remained intact and as she writes in her bestseller, *My Stroke of Insight*, "I was not capable of deliberating about past or future-related ideas because those cells were incapacitated. All I could perceive was right now, and it was beautiful."

Author Janet Ungless wrote about Dr. Taylor's experience in the May 2013 issue of Prevention Magazine. In the article Dr. Taylor gives us an interesting spin on her condition:

"This was the blessing I received from my experience: that nirvana is just a thought away—or, in my language [of science], deep inner peace exists in the consciousness of our right hemisphere. And at any given moment, you can choose to hook into that part of your brain, into a peaceful state, if you are willing to stop the cognitive loops of thought, worry, [anger]— any ideas that distract you from the experience of being in the here and now. What my stroke did was shut out all those moments; it silenced the dominating, judging voice of my left mind. And when that happened, my consciousness dwelled in a flow of sweet tranquillity.

You have to be willing to come to the present moment and set your ego aside—she's not going anywhere. You can go back and pick up where you left off. Our desire for peace must be stronger than our attachment to our misery, ego, or need to be right. It's about paying attention to your thoughts, watching what's going on inside your mind and observing it instead of engaging with it. What this is, essentially, is mindfulness."

Mindfulness. Not our usual mindlessness.

Remember that gap that we mentioned with our *Pattern Interrupt*? This comes from Katherine Ellison's excellent *Psychology Today* article "Mastering Your Own Mind:"

"For most of us, the lag time between provocation, impulse and action is shorter than a heartbeat—just a quarter of a second between the trigger event and the response of the amygdala, or fear center. In that fraction of a second, our emotions have time to swamp our judgment—and often do.

Meditation, however, promises to break this apparent chain reaction by allowing us to recognize "the spark before the flame." Through many hours of quietly observing the customary tyranny of the emotions, you may gradually familiarize yourself with the quiet of your mind—the part that one day might choose not to be tyrannized. Says Ricard, "You become familiar with the way emotions arise, how they can either overwhelm your mind or vanish without making an impact."

Mindfulness meditation has gone mainstream. It's no longer looked upon with apprehension. Although its roots are in

Buddhism, the actual practice can be quite secular. As a bridge to an actual seated mindfulness meditation practice, it may be easier to simply start with practicing mindfulness in your daily life.

You can choose any given moment to be mindful. It's being consciously aware of the present moment. Do it at a meal, in the shower or sitting in an incense filled room.

Smell the food before bringing it to your mouth, savor its taste rather than shoveling it down. In the shower feel the water splashing onto your skin. Warm? Cool? Hear it cascading over your body. All in the present moment. Without judgment. When thoughts come, as they will, let them pass. Be aware of your breathing. Be in the now.

Mindfulness is "the intentional, accepting and non-judgmental focus of one's attention on the emotions, thoughts and sensations occurring in the present moment."

Dr. Taylor observed from her stroke that:

"Because we're biological, we think of ourselves as these mushy, biological things. But if we look at ourselves as circuit boards, as computers, things become simple to understand. The brain is circuitry, and with circuitry, you can choose to run it—or not. I can run a program, whether it's my emotional programming or my intellectual programming, because I have cells that perform those functions. When you allow yourself to step outside the circuitry, then you're no longer consumed by it, and you're no longer forced to [do what it wants you to do].

We can consciously influence the neural circuitry underlying what we think, how we feel, and how we react to life's circumstances. Before my stroke, I thought I was a product of my brain. I had no idea that I had some say in how I responded to the emotions surging through me. "Fear" is just circuitry—False Expectations Appearing Real. You can choose to hook into it or not. It's a story that [your] left brain chatter circuitry is running—what if, what if, what if—but if you know that your brain chatter is just a tiny little group of cells, then they have no power. You can choose not to listen to them, and tune in to the present moment."

"Fear" is just circuitry. *You* are in charge. Turn the switch.... Or not. **Tune into the present moment.**

Be here now.

Empowering, is it not?

MENTAL HACK NINE ACTION STEPS: Read the entire Prevention article by Janet Ungless:

In a search engine type "Prevention Magazine A Stroke Of Enlightenment By Janet Ungless" (without quotation marks).

Watch/listen to Jill Bolte Taylor's TED talk:

At *Ted.com* in the search bar (upper right hand corner - magnifying glass) type "My stroke of insight".

Read Katherine Ellison's excellent *Psychology Today* article:

In a search engine type "Psychology Today Mastering Your Own Mind by Katherine Ellison".

SYMBOLS

A symbol is something that stands for something else. A complex concept can immediately flash into your consciousness by a word, sound, gesture, physical object or visual image.

Your name is a symbol of *you*. If I showed you a red octagon shaped symbol, you would instantly know its meaning is "STOP". And, if I type: I ♥ New York, well, you know my meaning.

There are mathematical symbols such as + and - as well as symbols used in its various branches such as [x] in algebra and π in geometry. Medicine and the sciences all have their symbols and let's not forget the super-secret handshake of those secret societies.

Joseph Campbell was the guy whose work in mythology influenced George Lucas' creation of *Star Wars*. Pretty cool guy, huh? In his essay *The Symbol without Meaning* he explains that a symbol can have a powerful effect on our psyche. He tells us that *"a symbol is an energy evoking, and directing, agent."*

If you so choose, you are about to participate in an experiment. Did any of these **Mental Hacks** give you an *aha! moment*? The notion that *I never thought of it like that before* or *I never looked at it from that angle?*

On the page preceding each **Mental Hack** is a symbol. Each was created with a single purpose in mind. To encompass the meaning of the text that follows. If that text sparked an inspirational idea in you then you can use it as *an energy evoking, and directing, agent.*

Copy the **Mental Hack symbol** that gave you the inspiration. If it was more than one, choose that one that gave you the greatest burst. Reread the **Mental Hack** while glancing at the printed copy of the symbol. Do this several times a day for a period of thirty days. The idea is that when you look at the symbol the entire concept should fill you consciousness. Make it a ritual so that, like looking at that red octagon, you don't have to think. Because you know.

Keep your copy of the symbol near you at all times. Laminate it and use it as a key chain if you'd like. Put one in, or on, your desk. Keep it in your purse, in your pocket, on your person. And when the next panic attack strikes you now have a secret weapon. Don't underestimate the power you can bring to this.

Good luck! Freedom awaits you.

MENTAL HACK TEN ACTION STEP: Download your symbol from Ihadapanicattack.com/symbols and start your thirty day experiment.

AFTERWORD

My hope is that I have been able to illustrate for you some different ways to "see" your panic attacks.

What we think of as our reality is influenced by our *interpretation* of incoming stimuli. The Wizard of Oz, Darth Vader, the *boogeyman* and yes, your panic attacks, are not who or what they appear to be. There is a facade that hides their true selves. A masquerade, an illusion that you perhaps were able to peek behind.

Francis Bacon declared "knowledge is power." Use this knowledge. Your life is important and you can be so much more without the awful burden of panic attacks.

You may have heard some or all of these "Mental Hacks" before. Maybe told in a different way. Sometimes we listen but we don't really hear. I know it's true for me.

Sometimes we use binoculars when a microscope is more appropriate.

Our thoughts lead us in one direction when the other would be of greater benefit.

Take a look at this drawing:

What do you see? A woman seated at a vanity table? Or perhaps you see the skull (you may need to look at this from a distance to see it.)

You can control your mind if you choose to. And it's your choice on what you focus.

Will you let your habits control you?

When a panic attack strikes you now, you have some tools that you can use. But it takes effort. I hope you'll give it a try.

The Beginning of the End?

I don't expect that this small group of **Mental Hacks** will help everyone. My hope is that it will help a few. Even one will do. Especially if that one is you!

You may have to work on it for awhile. This isn't something you plug in and let run on autopilot. You have to take an active part. If you won't do it, who will?

It's a challenge. Make it exciting.

If this has helped you in any way, I would appreciate hearing your results in a review. And if you hated it, let me know that too, and why. Maybe I can improve it for others.

Either way, my very best to you on your journey of imagining your panic attacks as a thing of the past.

APPENDIX:
MENTAL HACK ACTION STEPS

I Think, Therefore I Am... Afraid

MENTAL HACK ONE ACTION STEP: Think of at least two times when *your* thoughts caused your feelings.

Dog Training 101

MENTAL HACK TWO ACTION STEP: Think of specific actions you take throughout your day that are actually re-actions.

Fighting Fire With Fire

MENTAL HACK THREE ACTION STEPS: Think of how you react to a panic attack. Is it the same way each time? Have you ever devised a plan to "fight back"? You are being "attacked" after all.

Watch as a young agoraphobic woman confronts her fear of elevators during a session of Intensive Exposure Therapy:

https://www.youtube.com/watch?v=wE5F-FjbTRk

Rocky vs The Karate Kid

MENTAL HACK FOUR ACTION STEPS: Get some inspiration from Frank Costanza and De Niro's Travis Bickle (WARNING: Adult language!)

https://www.youtube.com/watch?v=LpJOxbaC8YU

https://www.youtube.com/watch?v=hSbtDuFJF6U

The Beatles vs Bizarro World

MENTAL HACK FIVE ACTION STEPS: Think of how you can react differently at the onset of your next panic attack in order to break an habitual cycle.

Listen to Jim Malone's Chicago Strategy:

https://www.youtube.com/watch?v=2ScvAJG51V4

Tell Spock It Worked

MENTAL HACK SIX ACTION STEPS: Watch what happens when an alien takes over the Enterprise and how it is defeated:

https://www.youtube.com/watch?v=_v698nFlAVw

Does your panic attack look like this alien:

https://www.youtube.com/watch?v=_ZgWBpWnxk4

Time to see the light:

https://www.youtube.com/watch?v=Bi3-CEbsxvA

What does your panic attack LOOK like?

Alchemical Magic

MENTAL HACK SEVEN ACTION STEP: Use your imagination to come up with an exciting scenario that you can use to transmute your next panic attack.

Please ~~Don't~~ Interrupt

MENTAL HACK EIGHT ACTION STEP: Devise your two *Pattern Interrupt* scenarios. One for when you're in the public and one when you're alone.

Be Here Now (or at least by next Tuesday)

MENTAL HACK NINE ACTION STEPS: Read the entire Prevention article by Janet Ungless:

http://www.prevention.com/mind-body/emotional-health/how-stroke-led-one-brian-scientists-enlightenment

Watch/listen to Jill Bolte Taylor's TED talk:

http://www.ted.com/talks/jill_bolte_taylor_s_powerful_stroke_of_insight?language=en

Read Katherine Ellison's excellent *Psychology Today* article:

http://www.psychologytoday.com/articles/200608/mastering-your-own-mind

Symbols

MENTAL HACK TEN ACTION STEP: Download your symbol from Ihadapanicattack.com/symbols and start your thirty day experiment.

Made in the USA
Las Vegas, NV
10 December 2022